T0303589

Together Now

Alfonso Zapata

poems

BELLE POINT PRESS

Fort Smith, Arkansas

Together Now: Poems

Cover image: Getty Images via Canva Pro License

Edited by Casie Dodd
Design & typography by Belle Point Press

Belle Point Press, LLC
Fort Smith, Arkansas
bellepointpress.com
editor@bellepointpress.com

Find Belle Point Press
on Facebook, Substack,
and Instagram (@bellepointpress)

Printed in the United States of America

28 27 26 25 24 1 2 3 4 5

ISBN: 978-1-960215-21-5

CHAP13/BPP31

Contents

In memory of Alfonso Zapata Sr., Papi Poncho
1942–2023

Como me Duele

After Selena: Live From The Astrodome *(1995)*

wringing runs from *perder*, she lives
in my padrinos' playlist, synths shining

she's twenty-three here so that's
the version that we get to remember

her voice slick as gliss, bookending
bassline slides, chords chopped close

guitarists, singers, drummers in all black
to let her explode in front of them

here with tio's silver piped shirts
gut scrubbing polish off belt buckle tops

her immortal cross chest glowing unfaded
magenta, this dress a Halloween costume

she sings, we laugh at card games, bad plays
grandparents yell about my sloppy shuffles

her family band knows they're out
of focus for the broadcast, for her stage

hands unable to form the bridge
on their own, over Selena's last song

sixty-seven thousand pairs of ears circling
the performers, all tuned to her finale

but she is far from this moment. we know
she's dead in a month but here it's different

she doesn't know yet, so as cymbals
shatter she shouts *hasta luego*, see you later

the little details are what we have to latch onto;
a bandaged index, her husband's showoff solo

and now there's a grimness behind the firework
pop and flash, smoke wafting as she waves to us

we will always interrupt ourselves
to reanimate her; when she says *ayudame*

help me, I know loss, I know pain
you do too, say it with me, con animo

she means us, we'll drop conversation
to come to her, to be her voice, together now:

ay ay ay, como me duele

Debut

For the 27th Anniversary of D'Angelo's Brown Sugar

Praise the Montgomery Ward
Aiwa my mother spent
her first paycheck on, thrumming
with D'Angelo, brown sugar

a lull for prenatal-me, a bassline blessing
across every amniotic ripple. Colic
was my condition, cured by track two.
His falsetto reached, alright,

over terrible twos and threes, soulful
whine masking mine. If your voice
can't sound that good, why bother
talking at all? *Jonz in my bonz*

was an early search on dad's eMachine,
aged four, a Google Image education,
bodies in an 800x600 spread for me.
Finally those dreaming eyes of mine

open up, I begin to see and make sound
again, muted like cupped trumpets.
Now is a time of contrasts, five rests
for each sound. *Shit, Damn, Motherfucker,*

in that order, were my first swears, a habit
forming drug, curses clattering out
of my mouth like snare snaps in sixth grade
classrooms, coarse language from smooth

faces. It was seven years ago that I
shifted from short story, lured from
Flannery to the song of individual
words, practicing assonance, cruising

across colonies of consonants.
Writing, song, art has been an act
of finding out how we sound again.
On that eighth day, when we get by,

when we are new again, words will
emerge sturdy from behind our canines.
We'll know how we carry music and vice
versa along the way, from grace and malady,

everything influential as decimals.
Line lengths like mixing boards,
I step up to the microphone believing
from here it only gets higher.

Palm Reading

I wish I was an NBA player because then I'd never
have to wonder what to do with my hands
in a picture but here I am palm sweat pooling
in the lithe curves of a keyboard beading on *I*
I shake people's hands and venture into their skulls
to see instinctive flinch tongue scraping the backs of teeth
as they wipe their hand on their leg *sorry about that*
I stand fidgety because I have a rotation:
fold arms until the sleeve and side darken
pocket them like something illicit until wallet softens
rest them on thighs until their shadow sticks
after moving rinse with cold water repeat
and other times the medication works to crag
my skin dehydrating until lifelines are ravines
and I wonder what rough future a palm reader
would tell for me do they see that when I write
the words appear smeared and bleed
on my hand heels and notebook lines blur
making me the medium credited on placards
as *Damp Canvas?* But I can stop this spiral
because what we make mimics us
like transmission towers' raised arms
like cars and their eyes and ears
like trimmed trees part for power lines.
Every awkward affliction a collage of reason,
my writing comes from all these limbs.

Dendrochronology and the Art of Notetaking

I have taken the ballpoint pen
for granted. When it was all
quills and inkwells, every flourish
was an effort, an extra viscous dip
and risk of blotting your blotter.
I have the privilege of not thinking

about the curls of my I's, a drawstring
snap turning a T into one stroke,
these free fixations distinct like fingerprints.
We varicose notebooks, carve them
like tree rings and commit to a memory,
the way dog-eared novels diagnose

the past. *This ring tells of a wildfire*
decades ago; this fold tells of a reader
so startled by a revelation that the book
had to be put down for the night.
These pages, corners folded and greased
with palm sweat and cat spit,

will end up a bargain in an estate sale,
our little habits, unthoughts, outlasting
us the way a great grandparent
will soon only be
remembered by the scent
of their perfume

Leaving My Abuelos' Basement, Christmas Eve 2022

Accompanied by Cielito Lindo Huasteco

It's cold down here
but this is where we kids go

every cousin squeezed in
to cracked plastic children's chairs

we talk with wide gestures
swing inked arms wild

to liven the place up.
Bass once bled

through the drop ceiling
my tia's buzzed cackle

rattling through the vent
the playlists are softer now

papi poncho heads to bed at nine
we pull him up, he trails

his oxygen tank to the door for the night.
When dinner's done we step upstairs into the clouds

of masa harina and the sweat stuck kitchen
shake thin salt from little roosters

singe fingertips peeling tortillas
from greased comals

nestle rice onto hot pot holders
ignore the living room's new bedpan.

Cielito Lindo appears
as it always does

we sing *ay ay ay ay*

but now there's one fewer
in the chorus

and I imagine a quiet
swelling up

once midnight hits
we drive fifteen minutes home

I drive five hours home
and now I know how it feels

from the inside to watch
a band breaking up

Moving a Hospital Bed into the Living Room

It's supposed to be improvement,
break from the hospital's unfamiliar,
but it's only extension, long arm
reaching from examination room
to grandparents' house, reminder.
Still, we know he'll be happier home,
no matter how unwell it'll become.
So we let bulging wires trace walls
and weave between family photos
like deflating veins, infect the hallways,
turned sick and long. We adapt to the stick
of bedside-table rubber. Allow oxygen
tank permanent residence in the corner.
My grandmother will sleep on the couch
next to him, but won't let it become her bed.
Will always move pillows and blankets
from closet to sofa,
from sofa to closet,
believing that this
will be temporary.
I hoped she was right.

A Dedication

Admire the apple corer, the specific
tool: post-driver, wick cutter, rice
cooker and its slow rumble, the -ers
of single advertised use, how titles
seem to signify it all, how bits
of materials configured in such
a way can narrow their purpose
from infinite to one. Or so
the packaging says: the corer can
peel, a wick cutter can clip roaches,
titles just an assignment.

My grandfather, trying to bounce back
from pneumonia, tubed and tanked,
asks about the air pressure of my tires.

After telling me how thin I've become
since cutting back on the Blue Moon,
my grandmother hands me her bottle
of Corralejo, brown liquor in sapphire
and amber, to have me pour us shots.

The first time I understood
my father was a weekend
watching him squint through
a wet windshield's bokeh,

strap cargo against wind,
sink tent-poles into muck,
bail floodwater from his kayak,
was seeing him see it through.

My mother details the satisfaction
of a well-timed vacuum: the crackle
of dust and cat litter crammed into
plastic chambers, compressed into loaves,
fill, expunge, again, again, silence
the sign that it's finished, the way
an open book abandoned will close itself.

The -ers carry invisible weight,
cumbersome as design docs, hefting
them over bruising shoulders
to lighten loads. When we leave, the -ers
can become raw material again,
become an expanded infinite
carrying less and less every hour.
I ask of them one more thing: teach me
how to carry the weight someday too.
Stay hydrated, yes mother.
Lift with your legs, yes father.

The Ghazal I Asked For

After Larry Levis

I will light novels on fire, hold them high, let syntax drip
onto my chest, crisp like hot wax on skin, old burnt words

I will collect texture, take scuffs from brick, pull hangnails
Blindfolded, I will read like braille the world's hurt words

I will lie naked on wet gazettes, osmose an aria from touch
hope that it works; that on my skin there will lurk words

What to do with these words; arrange them? Play Tetris
with image, hold an adverb, flip familiar, overheard words?

I will work from taste, find my way from zest and stale air
I will sit at the edge of the bed. You will kneel: her words

I will hold until the moment to make something worth something
I learn to love pain, hope I have deserved or earned words

I will pull the words from my skin. I'll bind and sign them
Alfonso. I give you all I have, and now they're your words

Untitled

My name stretches three
before me. The one Zapata, a father,
roots transplanted carefully

by the second, hands brick
hard and red, from one country's
soil to another's, deep and black.

The third, a campesino hero,
bandoliered and dead young,
no blood between him and me

but the same starting point.
My family has never called me
Alfonso. It's reserved for the elders.

To them I'm AJ, grandfathered
initials, shortchanged a syllable
at Christmas parties.

And I, in classrooms, heard that name
called for attendance, after a long line
of names that blur,

last in the roll,
and it felt like
it couldn't possibly
be for me.

Leaving My Abuelos' Basement, Christmas Eve 2015

Accompanied by Cielito Lindo Huasteco

It's cold down here
but this is where we kids go

running out of seats on ever polished tile
leaning cool against wobbling wood walls

we cousins talk and I drone tired, sitting slouched
on an exercise ball after my Meijer shift

of scrubbing mold from produce misters
but energy buzzes from our cluster.

up there someone kicks a bottle
and stomps shake the drop ceiling

the circular tromps of someone trying
to dance with the jaunt of norteño.

mami la screams down *vente arriba*
y juga treinta y uno and slams the door

so I sling myself up those stairs
with all the other tired men because

who am I to refuse the slap
of hunched playing cards

on the still tacky lacquer of the table.
papi poncho is wired, thick mustache

freshly dyed in that too noticeable way
retired and refusing to stop wearing coveralls

and he offers the room, even me,
heavy glasses amber-tinted with tequila.

and as we sync at *ay ay ay ay*
canta y no llores

I take my first shot
with people who love me.

I'm offered licks of lime and salt
to soften the sizzle of sinuses

and the back jaw tingle but
I refuse because I want to be able

to get used to this, to be their type of strong,
to make this a tradition, to ascend

like all the other Alfonsos in the room,
to believe that we all will last

Interpreting Light

My mother, this son settled tight
in her body, didn't want my first light
to be artificial. So she brought us to the backyard.
Before the swingset and basketball hoop stood
like sundials, before the privacy fence parasoled

square feet in shade, there were only black lattices
of chainlink, yard blooming peridot. Here, I first saw
the half-light, the dawning galaxies of dandelion
and gnat swarm nebulae glimpsed through flesh.
She wanted to shock me, signal a Morse Code hello

months early to wake me from rest, to force me
to comprehend something. She touched her stomach,
transformed open fingers into blinds, ran them
between the light and me to cast barcode shadows
across forming eyes, flicking like fish eggs. I bristle

at the sentimental, the slow collection of overthoughts,
simple times filtered through a poet's selfish motives,
but permit me this moment of nostalgia for something
unremembered. Enough space has been partitioned
for the unknown of cosmos, let me lower the ceiling

for us both. I wonder what I saw: round bees clumsy
against wind, the doting arcs of powerlines, the untwisting
downward whirls of maple seed samaras? I wonder
if I saw anything at all, or if it was just the ends of shapes
dying at the doors of unbreached eyes

On Felling Sixteen Dying Trees

Another white pine leans after a wind-
storm whistles through split trunks

pinecones falling into floodwater
floating up and skirting dirty puddles

and dad's laid off this week so
he decides the whole treeline must go.

He points out trunks, flayed
nude, pockmarked and hollow, *now*

those holes aren't just on the outside,
they're all through them, these trees

are sponges and I don't want to get
sued when one tips over and hits a shed.

When we tear down the trees
every limb is sap stuck

forearms tacky with the stuff
pockets glued shut as each cut

coughs a last gasping phlegm.
He rents a woodchipper for the day, hands me

guide wires tied high as the ladder could reach
and I remember muscle, the dominant

chainsaw cutting wedges and my pull
toppling trees as old as him, as old

as his father when he was born.
We lift and slide them

into a mulching mouth.
In the still sore next week we ground

all the little stumps, erased traces
tracked roots like arteries

severed them with mattock swings
planted saplings.

We laid soaker hoses
staked fertilizer

both of us hoping
the new could survive

the storms longer than the old.

The Warmer the Wind

Wind blows the blind pull-string
into a guitar
and strikes a chord
I've never heard

Wind blows dried hornets
from their window
trap to land
in my damp hands

Wind blows warmer this winter
and we will say this
every year until
it parches our throats

Wind blows mold spores
from fuzzed leaves
in an attempt
at biological warfare

Wind blows slivers through
AC condensers
to slow erode
its whirring mimics

Wind blows in textures
to fan a tarot deck
and illustrates us
in unflattering flutters

Wind blows and we try
to echo it in our mouths
but only amount
to whispers

Wind blows and kicks up dust glinting
in amber sunlight
and animates
our fading shadows

Wind blows or breathes
four degrees hotter
and makes its point
to an empty room

Perishable Goods

Zip Code 43605: On January 6, 2022, an explosion from a nearby oil refinery shook my grandparents' house.

Since construction started in '70, Davis Besse Nuclear Power Station has had ten incidents.

If we are what we eat
then we were trash, a habit
of dumping Coke-sodden
ice, from paper cups, down
the sink. I consider what we

were afforded: canned foods,
Country Time from scrubbed
molé glasses. Iodide pills were free
for our proximity to Davis Besse,
but we were never afraid

of the nuclear, its radii.
We feared our breath.
Where we lived
there was always a fire
on the horizon, our sky

a scribbled slick, courtesy
of the refinery four blocks down:

the price of affordable housing.
We saw steel, its shine inked
away, and thought of our air,
thick enough to chew.

We feared the exhale of Ford
and Daimler-Chrysler
where our fathers burned
years and smoked metal, fumes
to create cars that create fumes,

feeding flames for bologna-
and-white-bread wages.
They waved off hard coughs,
our young eyes strong enough
to detect their uncertainty
in the lilt of an eyebrow.

My grandfather's
lungs depleted
my father earned
asthma we lived
days of algal bloom
of boil-water advisories
of great lakes dethroned
of drought and dry wells
of brush fires scraping numbers

off the backs of soccer jerseys
and we were lucky enough
to eventually leave, but
what's coming has everyone
in its doomed circumference.

I still hear the ice melting
in the sink, oblong shapes
losing grip and clinking
through U-bends, hear
where the water goes so
time is short. This is not
a lone nuclear family's
problem. I consider
what we're forced to swallow.
I consider what we're forced
to make our children inhale
to pay for our next breath.

Leaving My Abuelos' Basement, Christmas Eve 1999

Accompanied by Cielito Lindo Huasteco

The cold of the first one I remember
is a frozen moment, posed photos

of children waiting to be taken
in pastel chairs smiling lost-tooth grins

we're shining hands passing SNES controllers
we jump with Mario hoping we'll fly with him

here the ceiling is cosmically tall
we leap to reach its moon crags

and graze heaven with fingernails
in the basement where I was

conceived, where I was *not*
an accident but a surprise

to young parents deep in bottles.
I feel like I've never left here

like I never want to, but I'm hand held
hoisted over a shoulder up steep stairs.

Every Alfonso is Poncho but I
am not Alfonso. I'm AJ, or *ay-yay*.

Alfonso is reserved for men with creased eyes
with soul-patches with darkened hands.

They sing in a language I will not be taught
drink from fizzed bottles I can't touch

I sit on the laps of these gods and am told
one day mijo, one day, like divinity can be earned

and I cry imagining poncho, wondering
what happens to one when another ascends.

They sing and I don't know the words yet
but I know *ay ay ay ay* and the rest

seem to mean everything to them.
Canta y no llores

por que cantando se alegran,
cielito lindo, los corazones.

At midnight we walk home in the dark
and its moonlit snow to sleep

imagining glasses waiting to be filled
names ready to be emptied and earned

Acknowledgments

The poems "The Ghazal I Asked For," "Leaving My Abuelos' Basement 2022," and "Leaving My Abuelos' Basement 2015" first appeared in *Sho Poetry Journal*, Vol. 3.

The author would first like to thank his parents, without whose exhausting encouragement, and love, this work would never have come to pass. He would also like to thank Yusuf Akman, Kate Arden, Willie Carver, DaMaris Hill, NitaJade Jackson, Lucy Jayes, Julia Johnson, Clay Shields, Frank X Walker, Deidra White, and Jazmin Witherspoon for keeping him in the basement and pushing his work further and further in workshops and beyond. Finally, he would like to thank JTM for getting this whole thing started in the first place.

Alfonso Zapata is a poet living in Lexington, Kentucky. He received an MFA in poetry at the University of Kentucky and has attended the University of Toledo and the University of Southern Mississippi, where he obtained a master's degree in poetry. He has previously received the Jim Lawless IV Poetry Prize, and the 2022 & 2023 University of Kentucky MFA Poetry Awards. His work has previously appeared in *Sho Poetry Journal,* and he can be found editing and re-editing already published poems in various coffee shops in the area.

Belle Point Press is a literary small press
along the Arkansas-Oklahoma border.
Our mission is simple: Stick around and read.
Learn more at **bellepointpress.com**.

BELLE
POINT
PRESS